Good News:
I like my brand new attitude!

By Deven Tellis, Ed.D

Copyright © by Deven Tellis

Published by Quintessential Publishing House, LLC
Birmingham, AL

All rights reserved, including the express right to reproduce this book or portions thereof in any form whatsoever, whether now known or hereinafter developed. For information, address Quintessential Publishing House, 1401 Doug Baker Blvd Birmingham, AL 35242.

This book may not be copied or reproduced without the express written permission of the authors or publisher. Author may be contacted via email at pennedbydrdeven@gmail.com.

Manufactured in the United States of America
ISBN: 978-1-7365605-4-9

FIRST EDITION -

Illustrations: Valeria Luzhanskaya

Editing: WesCourt Advisors

USA $14.99

DEDICATION:

To 'Oha' & 'Nella',
With all my love...

Always remember that your attitude determines your altitude. You have the power to choose how you see the world.

Acknowledgements:

Thank you to my husband, Bob, and those friends and family members who have provided a safe, supportive space for me to nurture my big dreams. I appreciate all of you!

Why can't we just **be thankful** to simply have a glass?

What if I fall off my bike?

GOOD NEWS:
I don't stay down.
I get back up!

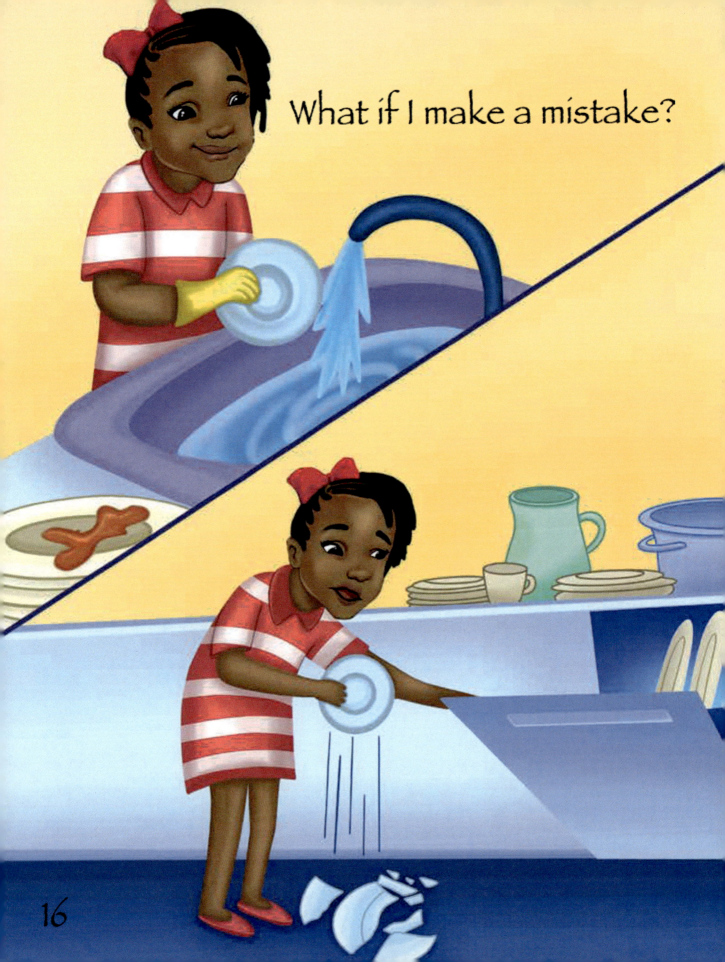
What if I make a mistake?

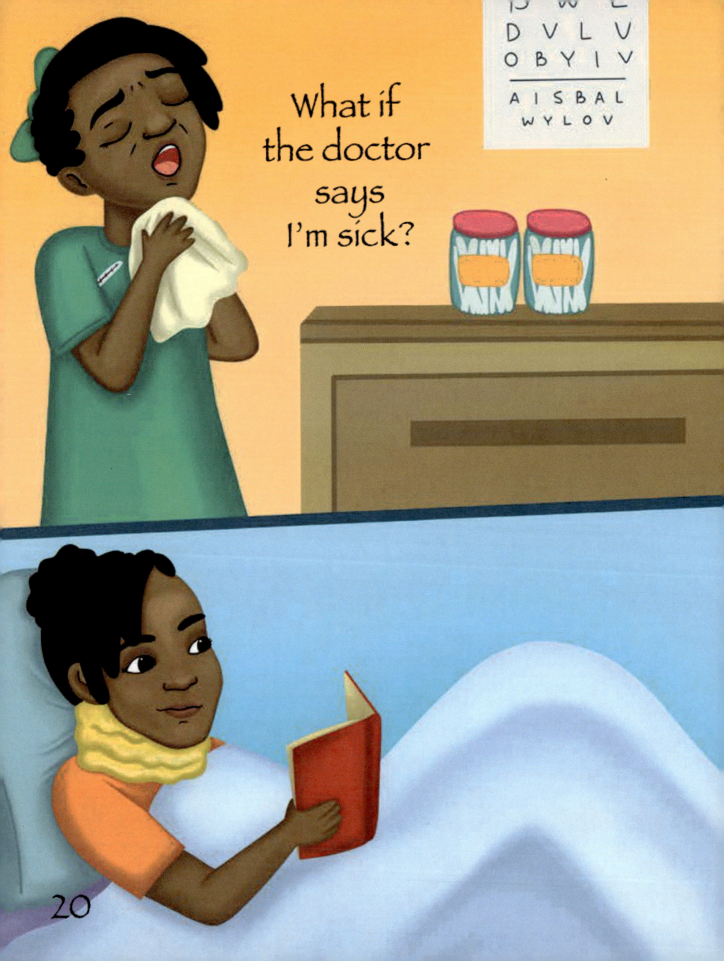

GOOD NEWS: I find comfort in knowing that

I'm mentally and spiritually strong.

What if I don't get everything I want?

GOOD NEWS:
I will be **thankful** that I do get what I need.

OTHER BOOKS BY THIS AUTHOR

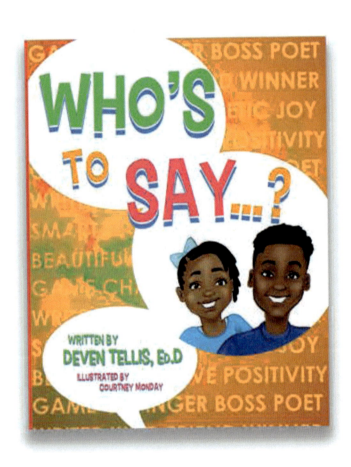
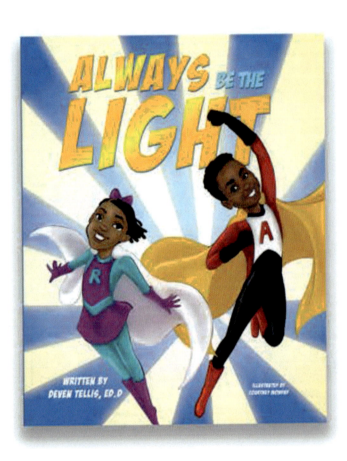

For more, Visit:
https://drdevencreates.com

Made in the USA
Middletown, DE
28 February 2023